Abraham Lincoln

Caroline Crosson Gilpin

NATIONAL GEOGRAPHIC

Washington, D.C.

For Kate, Meg, and John
—C. C. G.

Abraham Lincoln

The publisher and author gratefully acknowledge the review of proofs for this book
by Bryon Andreasen, Ph.D., Abraham Lincoln Presidential Library & Museum.

Library of Congress Cataloging-in-Publication Data
Gilpin, Caroline. Abraham Lincoln / by Caroline Gilpin.
   p. cm. ISBN 978-1-4263-1085-0 (pbk. : alk. paper)—ISBN 978-1-4263-1086-7 (library binding :
alk. paper) 1. Lincoln, Abraham, 1809-1865—Juvenile literature. 2. Presidents—United States—
Biography—Juvenile literature. 3. United States—History—Civil War, 1861-1865—Juvenile literature.
   I. Title. E457.905.G55 2013 973.7092—dc23 [B]
                                    2012031885

Design by YAY! Design

B/C: Bettman/Corbis; C: Corbis; GI: Getty Images; iS: iStockphoto; LC: Library of Congress Prints and Photographs Division;
SS: Shutterstock. Cover, Alexander Gardner/LC; cover (flag), Frank Jr/SS; 1, White House Historical Association; 2, SSPL/GI; 4 (top),
rsooll/SS; 4 (bottom), Voronin76/SS; 4-5, Ocean/C; 6, B/C; 7, MPI/GI; 8, C; 9, Raymond Boyd/Michael Ochs Archives/GI; 9 (inset),
tele52/SS; 10 (top), Gjermund Alsosv/SS; 10 (bottom left), B Calkins/SS; 10 (bottom right), Walter Zerla/SuperStock; 11 (top), Susan
Montgomery/SS; 11 (CTR), Thinkstock LLC/GI; 11 (bottom), The Alfred Whital Stem Collection of Lincolniana Repository/Library of
Congress, Rare Book and Special Collections Division; 12, North Wind Picture Archives/AP Images; 13, tele52/SS; 14 (top left), Burton
Historical Collection, Detroit Public Library; 14 (top right), Aperture51/SS; 14 (bottom left), RoJo Images/SS; 14 (bottom right), Rich
Pedroncelli/AP Images; 14 (Background), Steve Collender/SS; 15 (top left), Anton Violin/SS; 15 (top right), R. Gino Santa Maria/SS; 15
(left center), National Geographic Society/C; 15 (right center), Brady-Handy Photograph Collection/LC; 15 (bottom), Seth Perlman/
AP Images; 16, Universal History Archive/GI; 17 (top), Mort Kunstler; 17 (bottom), Archive Photos/GI; 18, Hulton Archive/GI; 19 (top),
Alexander Gardner/LC; 19, Kean Collection/GI; 21 (top), Eduardo Luzzatti Buyé/iS; 21 (center), iS; 21 (bottom), tele52/SS; 22-23, Na-
tional Geographic Society/C; 24-25, Brady-Handy Collection/C; 25 (top), Universal History Archive/GI; 25 (bottom), tele52/SS; 27
(top), tele52/SS; 27, B/C; 29, Orhan Cam/SS; 30 (top), Alexander Gardner/LC; 30 (center), Kean Collection/GI; 30 (bottom), Brady-
Handy Photograph Collection/LC; 31 (top left), JustASC/SS; 31 (top right), B/C; 31 (bottom left), Peteri/SS; 31 (bottom right), Arthur
Wallace Dunn Papers/LC; 32 (top left), B/C; 32 (top right), National Geographic Society/C; 32 (left center), C; 32 (right center), Win
McNamee/GI; 32 (bottom left), Interim Archives/GI

Printed in the United States of America
12/WOR/1

Table of Contents

A Much-Loved President

Who's on the penny? And the five-dollar bill? It's Abraham Lincoln, the 16th President of the United States!

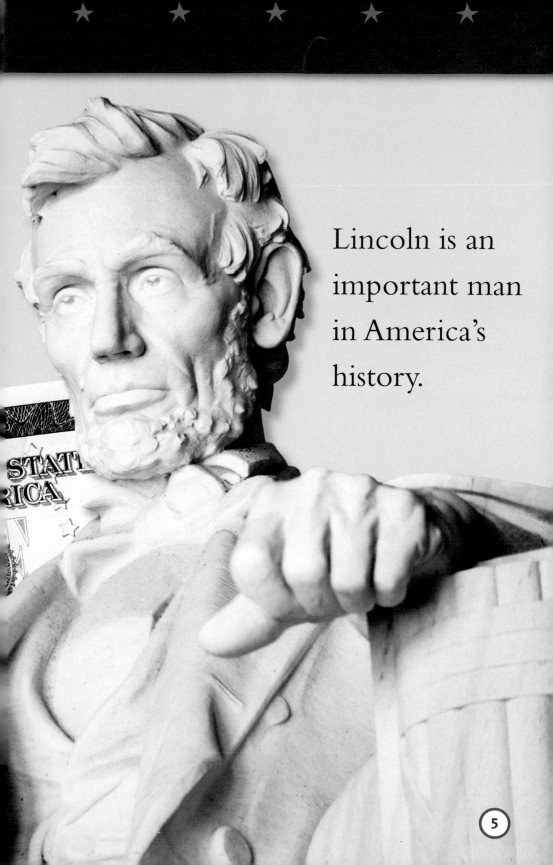

Lincoln is an important man in America's history.

A Country Boy

Lincoln was born in a one-room log cabin in Kentucky on February 12, 1809. He grew up in Indiana.

Lincoln read a lot of books.

Lincoln's family home in Kentucky

He wanted to go to school, but there was too much work to do on his family's farm. He chopped down trees, built fences, and plowed the land. He grew strong and very tall. Lincoln was kind and a good storyteller.

In His Own Words

"Leave nothing for tomorrow which can be done today."

Growing Up

All his life, Lincoln taught himself how to do things. He learned how to read and write, tell stories, and give speeches.

That's a Fact! Lincoln was an inventor. He had an idea for a machine to help ships float over sandbars.

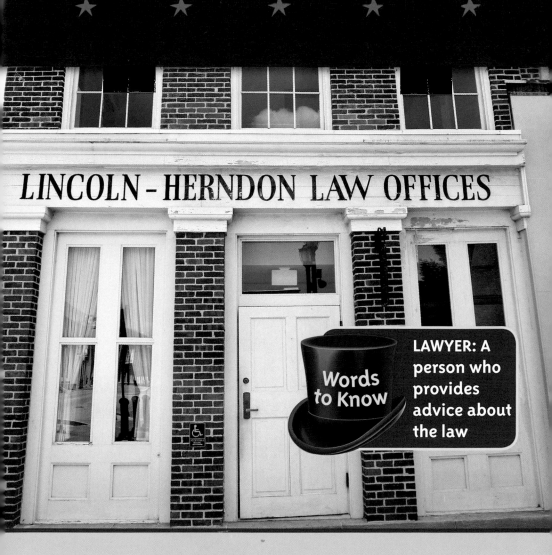

LINCOLN - HERNDON LAW OFFICES

Words to Know

LAWYER: A person who provides advice about the law

Lincoln learned how to fix machines. He taught himself how to pilot a riverboat and how to be a soldier. He even studied law and became a lawyer—all on his own.

In His Time

In the 1800s, many things were different from how they are today.

Money

A pair of shoes cost one dollar. A quart of milk cost ten cents. That doesn't sound like much, but dollars and dimes were worth a lot more back then.

Toys

In their free time, children played hopscotch and leapfrog. They also played with marbles, dolls, and toy trains.

School

Back then, not all children went to school. Those who did learned together in a one-room schoolhouse.

Transportation

People walked and traveled by horse-drawn carriages. Trains were used for long trips. There were no cars or airplanes.

U.S. Events

California became the 31st state in 1850. The *New York Times* newspaper started in 1851.

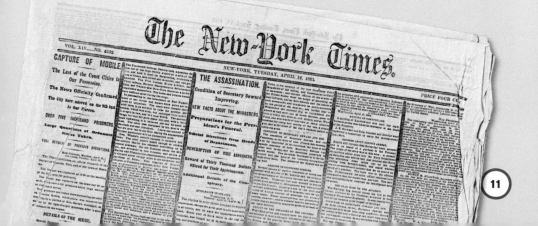

Becoming A Leader

In 1842, Lincoln married Mary Todd. They had four sons, named Robert, Eddie, Willie, and Tad.

A painting of the Lincolns with three of their sons, Willie, Robert, and Tad

That's a Fact!

Mary Todd was one of fifteen children in her family.

Lincoln was a good lawyer. People trusted him to make important decisions. So Lincoln became a politician (pall-uh-TISH-un).

Lincoln held two jobs as a politician for the state of Illinois. Then, in 1860, he ran for President. Lincoln won! He became the 16th President of the United States.

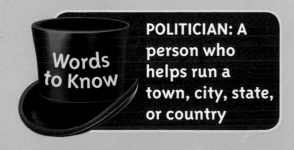

Words to Know

POLITICIAN: A person who helps run a town, city, state, or country

9 Awesome Facts

1

Eleven-year-old Grace Bedell wrote Lincoln a letter suggesting he grow a beard—and he did!

2

The Lincoln penny has looked the same since 1909, with Lincoln on the "heads" side.

3

Lincoln made Thanksgiving a national holiday in 1863. Magazine editor Sarah Josepha Hale suggested the idea to Lincoln.

4

Lincoln read the Bible often but did not belong to any church.

5

Lincoln owned horses, cats, dogs, and a turkey. Once, he saved his dog from drowning in a frozen river.

6

Some Presidents use speechwriters, but Lincoln wrote all his own speeches.

7

Lincoln's stepmother was an important person in his life. She encouraged him to read and learn.

8

Mary Todd Lincoln was more than a foot shorter than her husband.

9

Lincoln kept important papers in his stovepipe hat. This kept his head warm and his papers dry on rainy days.

Slavery

During Lincoln's time, some white people owned black slaves. The first slaves were brought to America from Africa. They were stolen from their families, and sold to people who used them to do work.

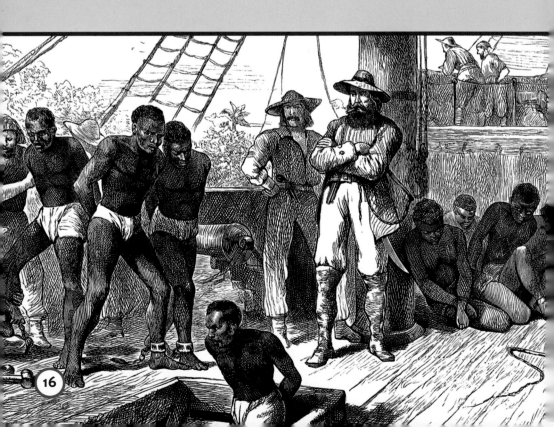

In His Own Words

"I want every man to have the chance — and I believe a black man is entitled to it—in which he can better his condition."

Slaves did not get paid and had to obey their owners. Slaves did not have any rights. They were often treated very badly. Many people were slaves because their parents were slaves. Those who tried to escape were often caught. Most slaves would never be free.

100 DOLLS. REWARD.
RAN AWAY
From me, on Saturday, the 19th inst.,
Negro Boy Robert Porter
aged 19; heavy, stoutly mad
dark chesnut complexio
sullen countenand

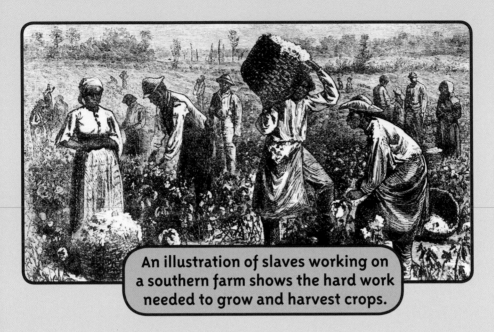

An illustration of slaves working on a southern farm shows the hard work needed to grow and harvest crops.

People all over the country disagreed about slavery. Many people in the South wanted slaves to work on their large farms. Most people in the North worked in cities and thought slavery was wrong.

That's a Fact!

Slaves used music for comfort and support. They sang about freedom, hard work, and their beliefs.

Lincoln was against slavery, and told people it needed to end.

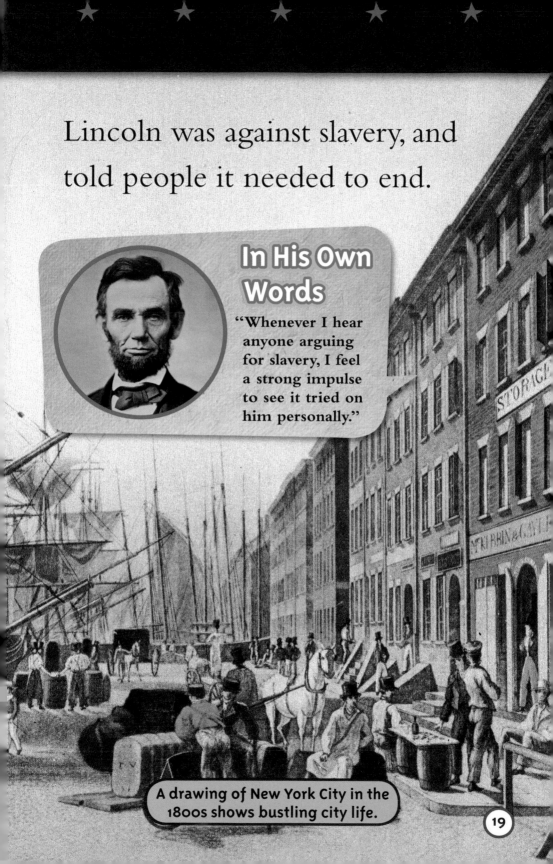

In His Own Words

"Whenever I hear anyone arguing for slavery, I feel a strong impulse to see it tried on him personally."

A drawing of New York City in the 1800s shows bustling city life.

Civil War

In 1861, 11 southern states broke away from the United States, which was also called the Union. These states did not want to be part of the Union because most of the Union wanted slavery to end.

The country began a long and bloody Civil War.

The West

Northern States

Southern States

Words to Know

CIVIL WAR: A war between people of the same country

THE UNION: The United States, but only northern states during the Civil War

Families disagreed and broke apart. Sometimes brothers fought on opposite sides. Some slaves escaped to the North to fight for freedom. Many people on both sides died.

In 1863, Lincoln freed slaves in ten states, but the war continued. Months later, he gave his most famous speech: the Gettysburg (GET-tees-burg) Address.

In His Own Words

"I say 'try'; if we never try, we shall never succeed . . ."

The Gettysburg Address

Abraham Lincoln stood on the battlefield where thousands had died to end slavery. He said that the country began with the idea that all people should be free. People listened to Lincoln's powerful words.

Abraham Lincoln at Gettysburg

In His Own Words

"Four score and seven years ago our fathers brought forth on this continent, a new nation, conceived in Liberty, and dedicated to the proposition that all men are created equal . . ."

—*The Gettysburg Address*

In 1865, after many more battles, the South surrendered. The North had won. The long, terrible war was over.

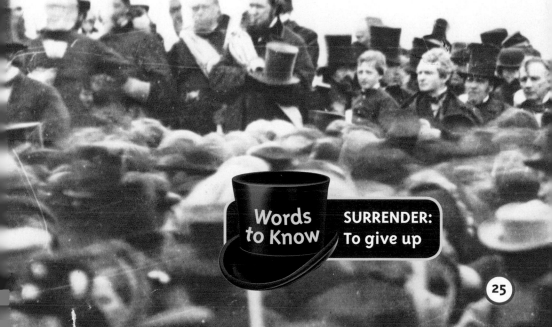

Words to Know

SURRENDER: To give up

Lincoln's Last Days

After the war, some Southerners were still angry. They didn't want Lincoln as President. A few were so angry they wanted to assassinate Lincoln.

On April 14, 1865, Lincoln went to the theater. During the play, he was shot by a man named John Wilkes Booth. Lincoln died the next day. Booth got away but was found and killed for his crime. Americans were sad to have lost Lincoln, their leader.

Words to Know

ASSASSINATE: To murder an important person

Lincoln's Life

Lincoln left behind a free country. The Union had been saved. Over time, Lincoln became one of the most loved of all American Presidents.

Each year, many people visit the Lincoln Memorial in Washington, D.C., and the Lincoln Presidential Library in Springfield, Illinois.

1809	1816	1830	1834	1842
Born in Kentucky to Thomas and Nancy Lincoln	Moved to Indiana	Moved to Illinois	Elected to Illinois State Legislature	Married Mary Todd

That's a Fact! The 36 columns of the Lincoln Memorial represent each state in the Union at the time of Lincoln's death.

Lincoln Memorial

When Barack Obama was sworn in as America's first black President, he used the same Bible that Lincoln used.

1846	1860	1863	1864	1865
Elected to U.S. House of Representatives	Elected President of the United States	Freed the slaves in ten states; gave the Gettysburg Address	Elected President for a second time	Died in Washington, D.C., on April 15

Be a Quiz Whiz!

See how many Lincoln questions you can get right! **Answers are at the bottom of page 31.**

1 Lincoln was the _____ President of the United States.
A. 4th
B. 16th
C. 10th
D. 1st

2 In Lincoln's time, _____.
A. Not all children went to school
B. People traveled by plane
C. People watched TV
D. Shoes cost ten dollars

3 What was Lincoln's wife's name?
A. Mary McDonald Lincoln
B. Marion Lincoln
C. Mary Todd Lincoln
D. Mary Adams

4

The night Lincoln was shot, he was at _____.
A. The White House
B. The theater
C. His family's farm
D. His law office

A slave _____.
A. Had to obey his or her owners
B. Was not paid for his or her work
C. Usually worked on large farms
D. All of the above

5

6

What is a war between people of the same country called?
A. A treaty
B. A civil war
C. A disagreement
D. A skirmish

How many sons did Lincoln have?
A. Six
B. Four
C. None
D. One

7

ASSASSINATE: To murder an important person

CIVIL WAR: A war between people of the same country

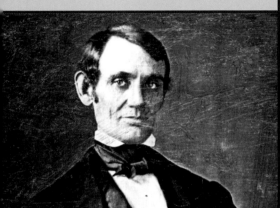

LAWYER: A person who provides advice about the law

POLITICIAN: A person who helps run a town, city, state, or country

SURRENDER: To give up

THE UNION: The United States, but only northern states during the Civil War